the
dog owner's
maintenance log

[olfactory sensor]

[optical sensors]

[exterior finish]

[tracking accessory]

[mood
indicator]

[excavation devices]

the
dog
owner's
maintenance log

A RECORD OF YOUR CANINE'S PERFORMANCE

by Dr. David Brunner and Sam Stall

Illustrated by Paul Kepple and Jude Buffum

QUIRK BOOKS

PHILADELPHIA

ALSO AVAILABLE

THE DOG OWNER'S MANUAL

ISBN 978-1-931686-85-3

A veterinarian for 25 years and operator of Indianapolis's Broad Ripple Animal Clinic for 22 years, DR. DAVID BRUNNER specializes in treating small animals—cats and dogs. He has two daughters, Molly and Kendell, two black Labrador retrievers, Lucy and Noel, and a wonderful cat named Mouse. He is also the coauthor of *The Cat Owner's Manual*.

SAM STALL is the coauthor of *The Cat Owner's Manual* and the author of *The Good, the Bad, and the Furry*. He resides in Indianapolis with his three terrier mixed-breeds, Tippy, Katie, and Gracie, as well as his wife, Jami (who has no terrier blood whatsoever), and their cat, Ted.

ISBN: 978-1-59474-046-6

Printed in China • Typeset in Swiss

Design and illustrations by Paul Kepple and Jude Buffum @ Headcase Design • headcasedesign.com

10 9 8 7 6 5 4 3 2

Quirk Books • 215 Church Street • Philadelphia, PA 19106 • quirkbooks.com

Contents

■ WELCOME TO YOUR NEW DOG! 7

■ OWNER'S RECORD 8

■ QUICK REFERENCE GUIDE 12

   Important Contact Numbers 17

   Vital Information 20

   Supplemental Visual Documentation 22

   Medication Record 26

   Vaccination Record 28

   Visiting Your Service Provider 30

   Canine Development Stages 32

   Spaying and Neutering 34

   Financial Records 36

■ ANNUAL PERFORMANCE EVALUATION 41

■ APPENDICES

   Audio Cues and Body Language 90

   Approximate Daily Fuel Requirements 92

   Calculating Age in Dog Years 94

   Technical Support 95

   Creating a Repair Kit 96

[front]

[left side]

[right side]

[back]

Welcome
to Your New Dog!

Congratulations on the acquisition of your new dog.

This product's legendary utility has inspired unprecedented customer loyalty among humans of every culture, age, and locale. With proper care and maintenance, it can accomplish almost any task you care to assign.

The dog is surprisingly similar to other high-tech devices you may already own. Like cars, dogs are available in numerous makes and models. Like PCs, they can be configured to serve many different functions. And like home security systems, they can keep you and your property safe and sound.

With proper guidance, this near-autonomous system can master numerous desirable behaviors. It can even provide companionship and love. All that's required is that you attend to its relatively modest programming, fuel, and maintenance needs. That's where *The Dog Owner's Maintenance Log* can be of assistance. This book is designed to serve as a convenient collection point for data on your model's development, medical issues, and much more. It also contains essential information on various dog-related matters that can help the novice owner solve common canine quandaries.

You'll find annual maintenance checklists for keeping track of the milestones in every year of your canine's service life. At the back of the log you'll also discover various primers on dog behavior, including tips on determining daily fuel requirements, how to calculate your canine's age in "dog years," and national organizations to contact for technical support. Store veterinary records and receipts, pedigree papers, and mementos in the convenient envelope.

Good luck—and enjoy your new dog!

Owner's Record

OWNER INFORMATION

| ○ Mr. ○ Mrs. ○ Ms. | First Name | Initial | Last Name |

| ○ Mr. ○ Mrs. ○ Ms. | First Name | Initial | Last Name |

| Address (Number and Street) | Apt. # |

| City | State/Province | Zip/Postal Code |

MODEL'S BIRTH DATE

☐☐ / ☐☐ / ☐☐☐☐

Month   Day   Year

MODEL'S ACQUISITION DATE

☐☐ / ☐☐ / ☐☐☐☐

Month   Day   Year

MODEL'S GENDER ○ Male ○ Female

MODEL'S NAME

| Casual Name | Pedigreed Name (If Any) |

MODEL'S DIMENSIONS

| Weight | Length | Height |

PLACE PHOTO HERE

DISTINCTIVE MARKINGS

EYE COLOR

○ blue   ○ brown   ○ gray   ○ green   ○ hazel

VENDOR SOURCE

INFORMATION ON PARENTS, IF ANY

Your feelings and feedback upon receipt and inspection of model

How many other similar products do you have in your house?

Name	Age	Species	Breed
Name	Age	Species	Breed

Breed Specification

CHECK ALL THAT APPLY:

- ❏ **Affenpinscher**
- ❏ **Afghan Hound**
- ❏ **Airedale Terrier**

- ❏ **Akita**

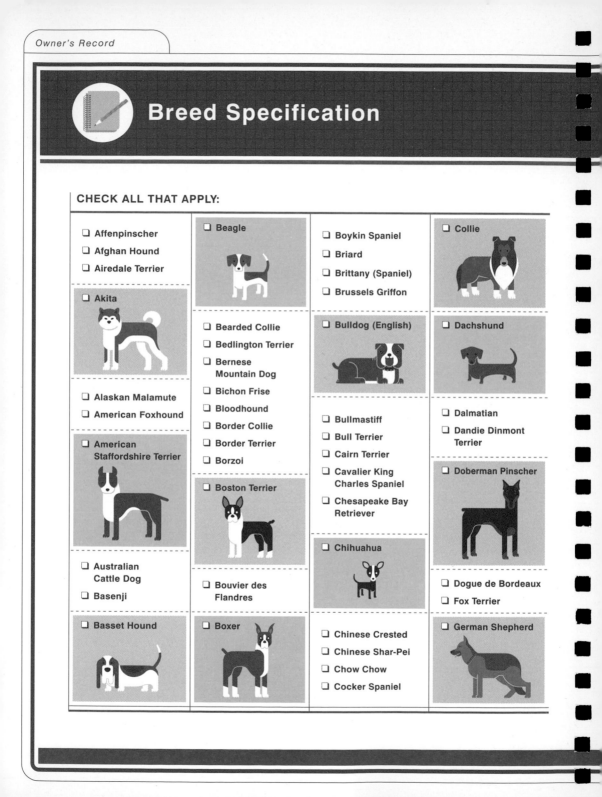

- ❏ **Alaskan Malamute**
- ❏ **American Foxhound**

- ❏ **American Staffordshire Terrier**

- ❏ **Australian Cattle Dog**
- ❏ **Basenji**

- ❏ **Basset Hound**

- ❏ **Beagle**

- ❏ **Bearded Collie**
- ❏ **Bedlington Terrier**
- ❏ **Bernese Mountain Dog**
- ❏ **Bichon Frise**
- ❏ **Bloodhound**
- ❏ **Border Collie**
- ❏ **Border Terrier**
- ❏ **Borzoi**

- ❏ **Boston Terrier**

- ❏ **Bouvier des Flandres**

- ❏ **Boxer**

- ❏ **Boykin Spaniel**
- ❏ **Briard**
- ❏ **Brittany (Spaniel)**
- ❏ **Brussels Griffon**

- ❏ **Bulldog (English)**

- ❏ **Bullmastiff**
- ❏ **Bull Terrier**
- ❏ **Cairn Terrier**
- ❏ **Cavalier King Charles Spaniel**
- ❏ **Chesapeake Bay Retriever**

- ❏ **Chihuahua**

- ❏ **Chinese Crested**
- ❏ **Chinese Shar-Pei**
- ❏ **Chow Chow**
- ❏ **Cocker Spaniel**

- ❏ **Collie**

- ❏ **Dachshund**

- ❏ **Dalmatian**
- ❏ **Dandie Dinmont Terrier**

- ❏ **Doberman Pinscher**

- ❏ **Dogue de Bordeaux**
- ❏ **Fox Terrier**

- ❏ **German Shepherd**

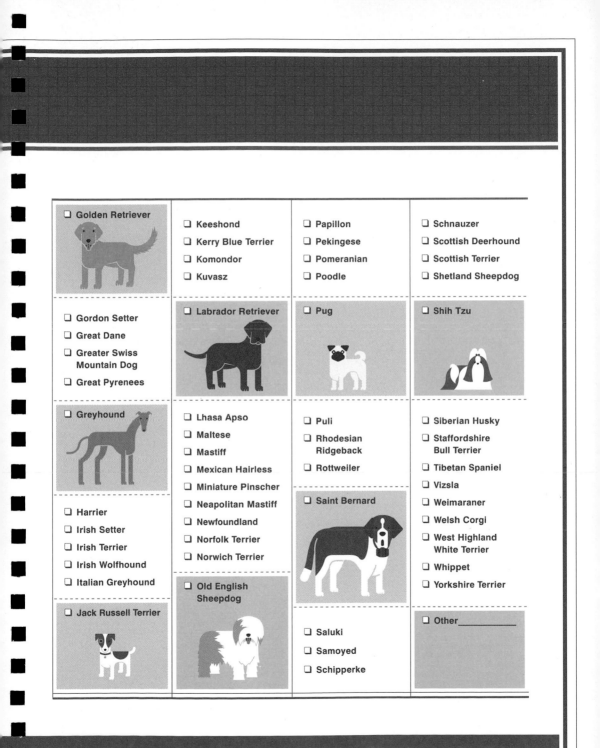

- ☐ **Golden Retriever**

- ☐ Keeshond
- ☐ Kerry Blue Terrier
- ☐ Komondor
- ☐ Kuvasz

- ☐ Papillon
- ☐ Pekingese
- ☐ Pomeranian
- ☐ Poodle

- ☐ Schnauzer
- ☐ Scottish Deerhound
- ☐ Scottish Terrier
- ☐ Shetland Sheepdog

- ☐ Gordon Setter
- ☐ Great Dane
- ☐ Greater Swiss Mountain Dog
- ☐ Great Pyrenees

- ☐ **Labrador Retriever**

- ☐ Pug

- ☐ Shih Tzu

- ☐ Greyhound

- ☐ Lhasa Apso
- ☐ Maltese
- ☐ Mastiff
- ☐ Mexican Hairless
- ☐ Miniature Pinscher
- ☐ Neapolitan Mastiff
- ☐ Newfoundland
- ☐ Norfolk Terrier
- ☐ Norwich Terrier

- ☐ Puli
- ☐ Rhodesian Ridgeback
- ☐ Rottweiler

- ☐ Siberian Husky
- ☐ Staffordshire Bull Terrier
- ☐ Tibetan Spaniel
- ☐ Vizsla
- ☐ Weimaraner
- ☐ Welsh Corgi
- ☐ West Highland White Terrier
- ☐ Whippet
- ☐ Yorkshire Terrier

- ☐ Harrier
- ☐ Irish Setter
- ☐ Irish Terrier
- ☐ Irish Wolfhound
- ☐ Italian Greyhound

- ☐ Saint Bernard

- ☐ Jack Russell Terrier

- ☐ Old English Sheepdog

- ☐ Saluki
- ☐ Samoyed
- ☐ Schipperke

- ☐ Other_____

Q U I C K   R E F E R E N C E   G U I D E : If any of these standard parts appear

THE HEAD

EYES: Most dog breeds come with brown or black eyes, though some varieties are fitted with blue, green, yellow, or even a combination of colors. Each optical device is equipped with three eyelids—upper, lower, and a "third" lid in the inner corner. The third lid functions as a "windshield wiper," clearing dust and debris from the surface of the eye.

EARS: May come in several styles, including button, floppy, and rose ears. The "erect ear" (seen on such brands as the German shepherd and huskies) is the standard type once used by all ancient dogs.

NOSE: As with the ears, the nose can take many forms and lengths. Colors can vary from black to liver; the color often lightens during winter. In general, the longer the nose, the more well-developed the dog's sense of smell. Its wetness increases its effectiveness by dissolving incoming scent molecules for analysis. Contrary to traditional beliefs, a dry nose does not necessarily indicate illness.

TONGUE: While frequently used to taste potential food, the canine tongue is also employed to vent excess heat. The movement of air back and forth across its surface (via panting), combined with the evaporation of saliva, serves to regulate body temperature.

TEETH: Dogs have 42 teeth, including six pairs of incisors in front that are bracketed by two pairs of large canines. The rest are molars and premolars, allowing dogs (unlike some predators) to easily add vegetarian fare to their diets if circumstances dictate.

to be missing or inoperative, consult your dog's service provider immediately.

THE BODY

OUTPUT PORT: The dog's waste discharge system also functions as a means of identification. The anus is bracketed by two internal anal glands that secrete a strong, pungent odor along with each bowel movement. This acts as an olfactory "calling card" to other dogs. When canines sniff each other's hindquarters, they are, in fact, investigating the anal glands.

COAT: All dogs, even the so-called "hairless" varieties, have a covering of fur. Its color and/or combination of colors can vary widely, even among members of the same breed. Muscles in the skin allow the hairs to stand up or "bristle." Excess shedding or a dull, brittle coat may indicate health problems.

GENITALS: Male dogs reach sexual maturity at approximately 8 months of age. Females become sexually mature at 9 to 15 months.

PAWS: Most of the dog's sense of touch is located here. Dogs can also sweat through their paw pads.

NIPPLES: These docking ports for peripherals come preinstalled on both female and male models. However, the circuitry of the male model renders these valves inoperative.

TAIL: Used primarily to signal emotions. The number of bones in a dog's tail (and therefore its length) varies from animal to animal.

WEIGHT: Dog weights vary markedly, from a minimum of 2 or 3 pounds (1–1.5 kg) to a maximum of more than 200 pounds (91 kg). In general, male dogs weigh about 10 percent more than females of the same breed.

HEIGHT: As with weight, canine dimensions vary widely from breed to breed. While the Irish wolfhound stands roughly 32 inches (81 cm) tall at the shoulders, the Chihuahua can be as short as 5 inches (13 cm).

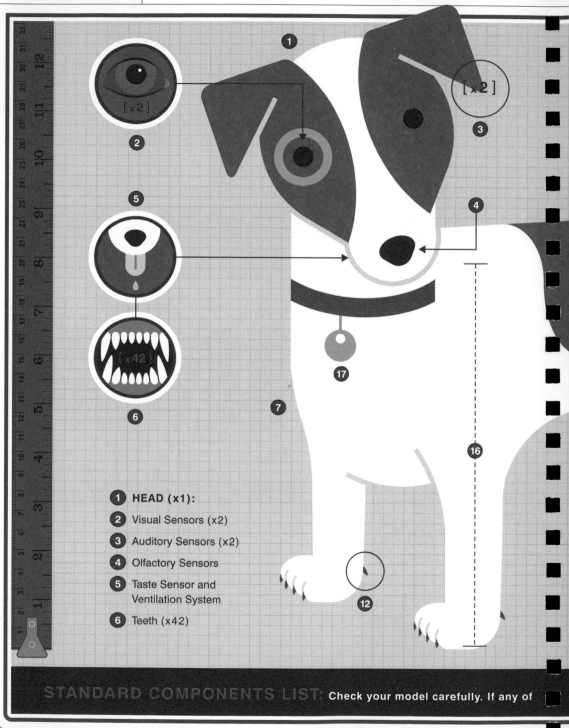

1. **HEAD (x1):**
2. Visual Sensors (x2)
3. Auditory Sensors (x2)
4. Olfactory Sensors
5. Taste Sensor and Ventilation System
6. Teeth (x42)

STANDARD COMPONENTS LIST: Check your model carefully. If any of

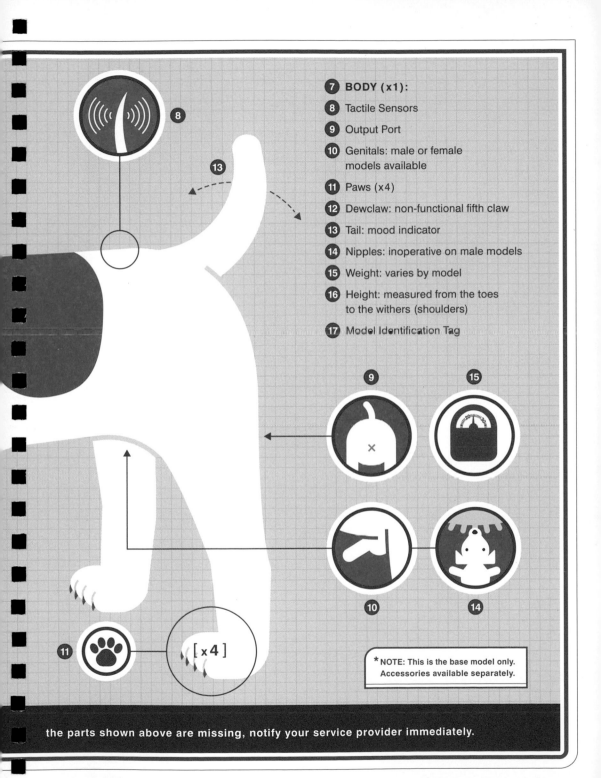

SENSOR SPECIFICATIONS

AUDITORY SENSORS: Dog ears can move independently of each other, allowing them to pinpoint the origins of specific sounds in a fraction of a second. Dogs can also hear extremely high frequencies (as high as 40,000 cycles per second, compared to 20,000 per second in humans) and detect noises at roughly four times the range of humans. In other words, what you hear at 50 feet (15 m), a dog can hear at 200 feet (60 m).

OLFACTORY SENSORS: While human noses contain between 5 million and 20 million scent-analyzing cells, dogs can carry 200 million or more. The bloodhound, famed for its tracking skills, possesses 300 million. To handle all this data, the olfactory processing center of the dog's brain is 40 times larger than that of humans. This faculty allows rescue dogs to detect humans buried under an avalanche and enables tracking hounds to follow scent trails that are three days old.

VISUAL SENSORS: The dog's vision is a legacy from the wolf. It is excellent for spotting moving targets at great distances and in poor lighting. However, dogs see fewer colors than humans and cannot discern fine detail. At close range they rely heavily on their sense of smell, which is almost unequaled in the animal world.

TACTILE SENSORS: Each hair in a dog's coat acts as an antenna, feeding environmental data to a mechanoreceptor nerve at its base. This data allows the canine to be acutely aware of its immediate surroundings.

TASTE SENSORS: Dogs possess only about 1,700 taste buds compared to roughly 9,000 in humans. This relative lack of taste explains their undiscriminating palates, allowing them to eat almost any food without complaint (and to lick themselves without gagging).

IMPORTANT CONTACT INFORMATION

PRIMARY VETERINARIAN:

Phone Number ⬜⬜⬜ – ⬜⬜⬜ – ⬜⬜⬜⬜ OFFICE
MOBILE

Phone Number ⬜⬜⬜ – ⬜⬜⬜ – ⬜⬜⬜⬜ OFFICE
MOBILE

Address

EMERGENCY OR AFTER-HOURS VETERINARIAN:

Phone Number ⬜⬜⬜ – ⬜⬜⬜ – ⬜⬜⬜⬜ OFFICE
MOBILE

Address

INSURANCE PROVIDER:

Phone Number ⬜⬜⬜ – ⬜⬜⬜ – ⬜⬜⬜⬜ OFFICE
MOBILE

Address

Policy Number

GROOMER:

Phone Number ⬜⬜⬜ – ⬜⬜⬜ – ⬜⬜⬜⬜ OFFICE
MOBILE

Address

IMPORTANT CONTACT INFORMATION

KENNEL:

Phone Number ☐☐☐ – ☐☐☐ – ☐☐☐☐ OFFICE
MOBILE

Address

DOGSITTER:

Phone Number ☐☐☐ – ☐☐☐ – ☐☐☐☐ OFFICE
MOBILE

Phone Number ☐☐☐ – ☐☐☐ – ☐☐☐☐ OFFICE
MOBILE

Address

ANIMAL SHELTER:

Phone Number ☐☐☐ – ☐☐☐ – ☐☐☐☐ OFFICE
MOBILE

Address

Web Site

ANIMAL POISON CONTROL CENTER:

Phone Number ☐☐☐ – ☐☐☐ – ☐☐☐☐ OFFICE
MOBILE

Address

CONTACT IN YOUR ABSENCE:

Phone Number [ ][ ][ ] – [ ][ ][ ][ ] – [ ][ ][ ][ ]   OFFICE
MOBILE

Relationship

Address

DOG'S BEST FRIEND:

Phone Number [ ][ ][ ] – [ ][ ][ ][ ] – [ ][ ][ ][ ]   OFFICE
MOBILE

Address

Canine's Parent(s)

OTHER:

Phone Number [ ][ ][ ] – [ ][ ][ ][ ] – [ ][ ][ ][ ]   OFFICE
MOBILE

Address

OTHER:

Phone Number [ ][ ][ ] – [ ][ ][ ][ ] – [ ][ ][ ][ ]   OFFICE
MOBILE

Address

VITAL INFORMATION: The data on these pages should offer a quick,

IDENTIFICATION INFORMATION

License Tag Number

Rabies Tag Number

Microchip Identification Number (If Any)

FEEDING

Specific Dog Food Brand

Portion Size

Number of Servings ○ ○ ○ ○ ○
                     1   2   3   4   5

Times of Daily Servings

#1 [ ] : [ ] AM/PM   #2 [ ] : [ ] AM/PM

#3 [ ] : [ ] AM/PM   #4 [ ] : [ ] AM/PM   #5 [ ] : [ ] AM/PM

Acceptable Snacks

Unacceptable Foods (If Any)

at-a-glance overview of the status of your model's hardware and software functions.

CHRONIC MEDICAL CONDITIONS

ALLERGIES (IF ANY)

Allergen	Symptoms
Allergen	Symptoms
Allergen	Symptoms

BEHAVIORAL QUIRKS

SUPPLEMENTAL VISUAL DOCUMENTATION

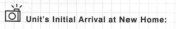

Unit's Initial Arrival at New Home:

First Exterior Grooming Session:

Memory Upgrade/Obedience Training:

Interactions with Family Members:

SUPPLEMENTAL VISUAL DOCUMENTATION

 **Holidays:**

Preferred Canine Associate(s):

Additional Documentation:

Medication Record

DATE	NAME	FUNCTION	DOSAGE

Medication Record

DATE	NAME	FUNCTION	DOSAGE

Vaccination Record

DATE	NAME	NOTES

Vaccination Record

DATE	NAME	NOTES

CAUTION

In certain regions of the world, additional vaccinations, such as for Lyme disease, may be recommended or required. Currently, there is much debate about which immunizations to administer and, most importantly, how often they can be safely given. Your veterinarian can perform a blood test, known as a "titer," to assess your canine's immunity to various infectious diseases (rabies, parvovirus, etc.) and determine whether booster shots are necessary. Consult him or her for recommendations and the latest data.

Barring emergencies, most dogs will require a handful of veterinary visits during their first year of life and annual visits thereafter. Listed below is an approximate guideline of when you should expect to have the dog serviced and what you can expect the veterinarian to do.

AGE 6–8 WEEKS

- Physical examination
- DHPP immunization (a combination vaccination for distemper, hepatitis, parainfluenza, and parvovirus)
- Stool exam for parasites

- Deworming
- Begin heartworm preventative medication and (if seasonally appropriate) flea preventative

AGE 10–12 WEEKS

- Physical examination
- DHLPP immunization (DHPP plus vaccination for leptospirosis)
- Deworming

- Kennel cough (Bordetella) vaccination, if applicable
- Administer heartworm preventative medication and (if seasonally appropriate) flea preventative

AGE 14–16 WEEKS

- Physical examination
- DHLPP booster immunization
- Rabies vaccination

- Administer heartworm preventative medication and (if seasonally appropriate) flea preventative

ANNUALLY

- Physical examination
- DHLPP booster immunization (consult your veterinarian as to its necessity)
- Kennel cough (Bordetella) booster, if applicable
- Rabies booster (if state regulations mandate). If not, every three years.

- Deworming (if necessary)
- Heartworm blood test
- Wellness testing in mature dogs (initiated at five to seven years to evaluate kidneys, liver, blood sugar, and other organ functions)

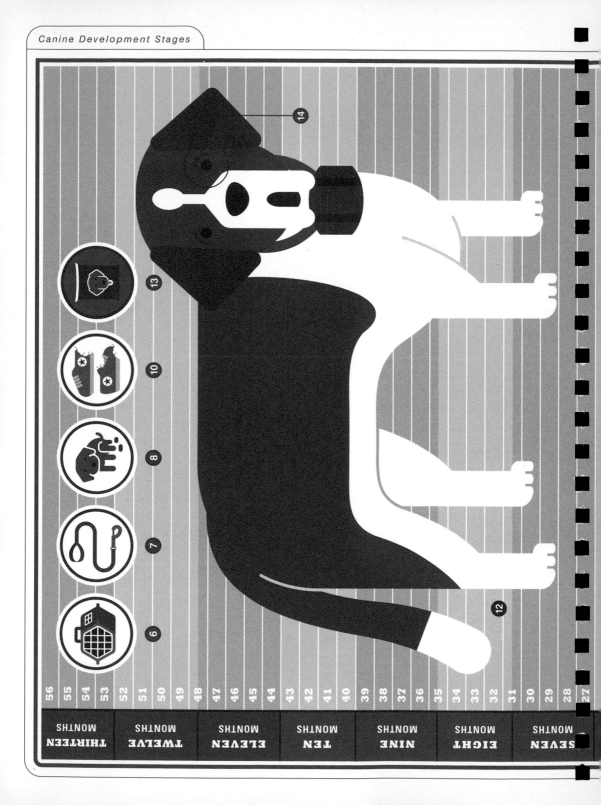

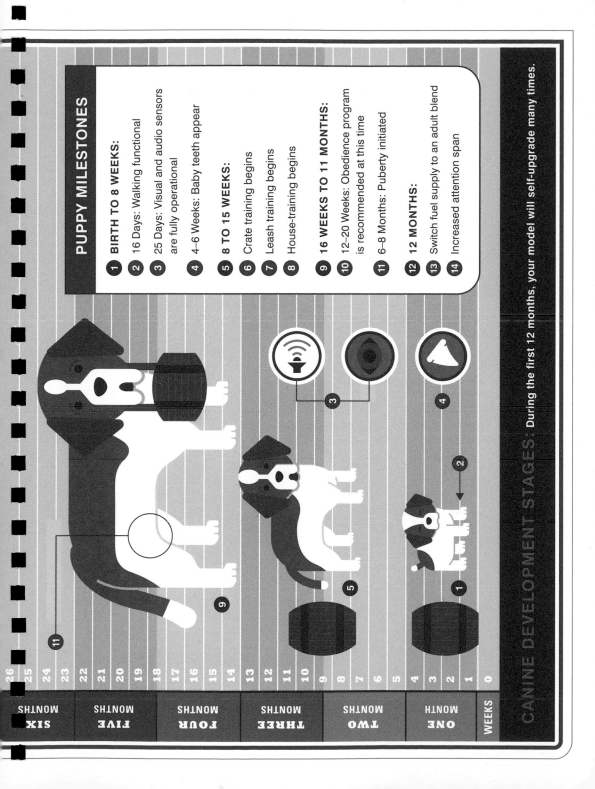

PUPPY MILESTONES

1 BIRTH TO 8 WEEKS:

2 16 Days: Walking functional

3 25 Days: Visual and audio sensors are fully operational

4 4–6 Weeks: Baby teeth appear

5 8 TO 15 WEEKS:

6 Crate training begins

7 Leash training begins

8 House-training begins

9 16 WEEKS TO 11 MONTHS:

10 12–20 Weeks: Obedience program is recommended at this time

11 6–8 Months: Puberty initiated

12 12 MONTHS:

13 Switch fuel supply to an adult blend

14 Increased attention span

CANINE DEVELOPMENT STAGES: During the first 12 months, your model will self-upgrade many times.

WEEKS	0
ONE MONTH	1 2 3 4
TWO MONTHS	5 6 7 8 9
THREE MONTHS	10 11 12 13
FOUR MONTHS	14 15 16 17 18
FIVE MONTHS	19 20 21 22
SIX MONTHS	23 24 25 26

Spaying and Neutering

**NEUTERING THE MALE
REDUCES THE RISK OF:**

1. Aggression
2. Prostate troubles
3. Testicular cancer

**SPAYING THE FEMALE
REDUCES THE RISK OF:**

4. Mammary cancer
5. Ovarian cysts
6. Uterine infections
7. Cancers of the
   reproductive tract
8. Unwanted puppies

It is the duty of every responsible pet owner to have his or her canine spayed or neutered. Unwanted litters contribute to a vast oversupply of dogs in the world. Unless you plan to breed your dog (which is not recommended, except in the case of highly valued purebred models), it should be sterilized before reaching sexual maturity. For males this is called *neutering* (removal of the testicles); for females, *spaying* (removal of the ovaries and uterus). Neutered males are generally less aggressive, less prone to roam, and less excitable than their unaltered peers. They also suffer from fewer health problems such as prostate troubles and testicular cancer.

Likewise, females spayed before puberty have their chances of contracting mammary cancer (an extremely common malady) reduced to near zero. Also, the danger of ovarian cysts, uterine infections, and cancers of the reproductive tract (all very common malfunctions) are eliminated. Neutered and spayed dogs tend to gain weight more easily, but this can be countered by feeding 10 to 20 percent less food and increasing exercise. In most cases, neutering and spaying can be performed at any time past the age of 16 weeks.

Financial Records

Use this section to create a financial "snapshot" of costs associated with the care, your choosing (three months, six months, a year) and then total them. If you find the

VETERINARY VISITS		
Date	Reason for Visit	Cost
		$
		$
		$
		$
		$
		$
		$
		$

VETERINARY PROCEDURES (surgeries, teeth cleanings, etc.)		
Date	Procedure	Cost
		$
		$
		$
		$
		$
		$
		$
		$

PET INSURANCE		
Year Policy Began	Policy Provider	Yearly Premium
		$

maintenance, and comfort of your canine unit. Simply record expenses for the time period of experience valuable, use these pages as a template for a financial record of your own creation.

MEDICATIONS		
Date Prescribed	Medication	Cost
		$
		$
		$
		$
		$
		$
		$
		$

FOOD (if necessary, estimate total expenditure)		
Date	Variety	Cost
		$
		$
		$
		$
		$
		$
		$
		$
		$
		$
		$
		$

Financial Records

GROOMING

Date	Name of Shop	Cost
		$
		$
		$
		$
		$
		$

KENNEL CARE

Date	Name of Kennel	Duration of Stay	Cost
			$
			$
			$
			$
			$
			$

OBEDIENCE OR OTHER TRAINING

Date	Nature of Training	Cost
		$
		$
		$
		$
		$

ACCESSORIES (toys, bedding, etc.)

Date	Description	Cost
		$
		$
		$
		$
		$
		$
		$
		$

MISCELLANEOUS

Date	Description	Cost
		$
		$
		$
		$
		$
		$
		$
		$
		$
		$
		$
		$

ANNUAL PERFORMANCE EVALUATION

Use the following pages to track the performance and operation of your canine. Be sure to document any visits to your service provider. You might also wish to note important events such as first car trip, the completion of house-training, any significant malfunctions, and so on.

YEAR 1

DATE ☐☐ / ☐☐ / ☐☐ through ☐☐ / ☐☐ / ☐☐

VACCINATION RECORD

☐☐ / ☐☐	Type	Information
Month / Day		

☐☐ / ☐☐	Type	Information
Month / Day		

☐☐ / ☐☐	Type	Information
Month / Day		

☐☐ / ☐☐	Type	Information
Month / Day		

MEDICATIONS

☐☐ / ☐☐	Type	Information
Month / Day		

☐☐ / ☐☐	Type	Information
Month / Day		

☐☐ / ☐☐	Type	Information
Month / Day		

MALFUNCTIONS

☐☐ / ☐☐	Type	Information
Month / Day		

☐☐ / ☐☐	Type	Information
Month / Day		

☐☐ / ☐☐	Type	Information
Month / Day		

Fleece toys are excellent for puppies. Adult canines appreciate hard rubber balls (choose one that is too large to swallow or become lodged in the dog's mouth). Avoid real bones, which may splinter, or household items such as shoes, which may convey the idea that all shoes are for chewing.

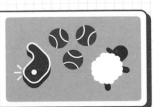

YEAR 2

DATE ☐☐ / ☐☐ / ☐☐ through ☐☐ / ☐☐ / ☐☐

VACCINATION RECORD

☐☐ / ☐☐	Type	Information
Month / Day		
☐☐ / ☐☐	Type	Information
Month / Day		
☐☐ / ☐☐	Type	Information
Month / Day		
☐☐ / ☐☐	Type	Information
Month / Day		

MEDICATIONS

☐☐ / ☐☐	Type	Information
Month / Day		
☐☐ / ☐☐	Type	Information
Month / Day		
☐☐ / ☐☐	Type	Information
Month / Day		

MALFUNCTIONS

☐☐ / ☐☐	Type	Information
Month / Day		
☐☐ / ☐☐	Type	Information
Month / Day		
☐☐ / ☐☐	Type	Information
Month / Day		

As with human adolescents, dogs entering puberty can experience some-times troublesome personality changes. Extra exercise, plus spaying/neutering before puberty, can help mitigate such difficulties.

YEAR 3

DATE ☐☐ / ☐☐ / ☐☐ through ☐☐ / ☐☐ / ☐☐

VACCINATION RECORD

☐☐ / ☐☐	Type	Information
Month / Day		
☐☐ / ☐☐	Type	Information
Month / Day		
☐☐ / ☐☐	Type	Information
Month / Day		
☐☐ / ☐☐	Type	Information
Month / Day		

MEDICATIONS

☐☐ / ☐☐	Type	Information
Month / Day		
☐☐ / ☐☐	Type	Information
Month / Day		
☐☐ / ☐☐	Type	Information
Month / Day		

MALFUNCTIONS

☐☐ / ☐☐	Type	Information
Month / Day		
☐☐ / ☐☐	Type	Information
Month / Day		
☐☐ / ☐☐	Type	Information
Month / Day		

Dogs have an easier time identifying a multisyllabic rather than a monosyllabic name. Consequently, *Rover* is better than *Spot*.

ROVER

YEAR 4

VACCINATION RECORD

☐☐ / ☐☐ Month Day	Type	Information
☐☐ / ☐☐ Month Day	Type	Information
☐☐ / ☐☐ Month Day	Type	Information
☐☐ / ☐☐ Month Day	Type	Information

MEDICATIONS

☐☐ / ☐☐ Month Day	Type	Information
☐☐ / ☐☐ Month Day	Type	Information
☐☐ / ☐☐ Month Day	Type	Information

MALFUNCTIONS

☐☐ / ☐☐ Month Day	Type	Information
☐☐ / ☐☐ Month Day	Type	Information
☐☐ / ☐☐ Month Day	Type	Information

Dogs, like wolves, mark the limits of their domain with urine and feces. This behavior greatly eases the process of house-training. Since dogs will repeatedly mark the same spots, pick a location in the yard where you want your pet to expel its waste. After the dog has used the spot a few times, it will update its internal preferences and remember the spot forever.

YEAR 5

DATE ☐☐ / ☐☐ / ☐☐ through ☐☐ / ☐☐ / ☐☐

VACCINATION RECORD

Month / Day	Type	Information
☐☐ / ☐☐		
☐☐ / ☐☐		
☐☐ / ☐☐		
☐☐ / ☐☐		

MEDICATIONS

Month / Day	Type	Information
☐☐ / ☐☐		
☐☐ / ☐☐		
☐☐ / ☐☐		

MALFUNCTIONS

Month / Day	Type	Information
☐☐ / ☐☐		
☐☐ / ☐☐		
☐☐ / ☐☐		

Pet insurance can help reduce the impact of unexpected maintenance costs. Just as with human health policies, owners pay a regular premium in exchange for assistance that ranges from coverage of annual checkups and immunizations to medical emergencies. Premium payments, which are based on services offered and the condition/age of the canine, can range from modest to expensive.

YEAR 6

VACCINATION RECORD

Month □□ / Day □□	Type	Information
Month □□ / Day □□	Type	Information
Month □□ / Day □□	Type	Information
Month □□ / Day □□	Type	Information

MEDICATIONS

Month □□ / Day □□	Type	Information
Month □□ / Day □□	Type	Information
Month □□ / Day □□	Type	Information

MALFUNCTIONS

Month □□ / Day □□	Type	Information
Month □□ / Day □□	Type	Information
Month □□ / Day □□	Type	Information

NOTES AND OBSERVATIONS

YEAR 6

On average, canine pregnancies last 63 days, though the duration can vary from 59 to 66 days. During pregnancy the mother's body weight may increase as much as 50 percent (a little over 30 percent is more typical).

53

YEAR 7

DATE ☐☐ / ☐☐ / ☐☐ through ☐☐ / ☐☐ / ☐☐

VACCINATION RECORD

☐☐ / ☐☐	Type	Information
Month / Day		
☐☐ / ☐☐	Type	Information
Month / Day		
☐☐ / ☐☐	Type	Information
Month / Day		
☐☐ / ☐☐	Type	Information
Month / Day		

MEDICATIONS

☐☐ / ☐☐	Type	Information
Month / Day		
☐☐ / ☐☐	Type	Information
Month / Day		
☐☐ / ☐☐	Type	Information
Month / Day		

MALFUNCTIONS

☐☐ / ☐☐	Type	Information
Month / Day		
☐☐ / ☐☐	Type	Information
Month / Day		
☐☐ / ☐☐	Type	Information
Month / Day		

Do not reprimand a dog for a transgression unless you catch the animal in the act of committing it. A dog will not understand that you are angry about something that it did an hour ago. It will simply know that you are angry—perhaps about what it is doing at the moment.

YEAR 8

VACCINATION RECORD

Month	Day	Type	Information
☐☐	☐☐		
☐☐	☐☐		
☐☐	☐☐		
☐☐	☐☐		

MEDICATIONS

Month	Day	Type	Information
☐☐	☐☐		
☐☐	☐☐		
☐☐	☐☐		

MALFUNCTIONS

Month	Day	Type	Information
☐☐	☐☐		
☐☐	☐☐		
☐☐	☐☐		

Snacks should compose no more than 10 percent of a dog's daily caloric intake. Appropriate snacks include commercial low-calorie dog treats, air-popped popcorn without butter or salt, broccoli, cooked green beans, and raw carrots.

YEAR 9

VACCINATION RECORD

☐☐ / ☐☐	Type	Information
Month / Day		

☐☐ / ☐☐	Type	Information
Month / Day		

☐☐ / ☐☐	Type	Information
Month / Day		

☐☐ / ☐☐	Type	Information
Month / Day		

MEDICATIONS

☐☐ / ☐☐	Type	Information
Month / Day		

☐☐ / ☐☐	Type	Information
Month / Day		

☐☐ / ☐☐	Type	Information
Month / Day		

MALFUNCTIONS

☐☐ / ☐☐	Type	Information
Month / Day		

☐☐ / ☐☐	Type	Information
Month / Day		

☐☐ / ☐☐	Type	Information
Month / Day		

Dogs, like humans, can become out of shape. Build up a sedentary canine's capacity slowly over weeks and exercise it daily, if possible. A canine can be conditioned with a 20- to 60-minute walk 5 days a week. Consult your veterinarian before beginning any sort of exercise program for an overweight, aged, and/or infirm canine.

DATE ☐☐ / ☐☐ / ☐☐ through ☐☐ / ☐☐ / ☐☐

VACCINATION RECORD

☐☐ / ☐☐   **Type**   **Information**
Month   Day

☐☐ / ☐☐   **Type**   **Information**
Month   Day

☐☐ / ☐☐   **Type**   **Information**
Month   Day

☐☐ / ☐☐   **Type**   **Information**
Month   Day

MEDICATIONS

☐☐ / ☐☐   **Type**   **Information**
Month   Day

☐☐ / ☐☐   **Type**   **Information**
Month   Day

☐☐ / ☐☐   **Type**   **Information**
Month   Day

MALFUNCTIONS

☐☐ / ☐☐   **Type**   **Information**
Month   Day

☐☐ / ☐☐   **Type**   **Information**
Month   Day

☐☐ / ☐☐   **Type**   **Information**
Month   Day

If a dog wants a treat or a toy, make it perform some trick or obey a command before providing it. This reinforces your authority over the canine in an easy, nonthreatening way.

YEAR 11

DATE ☐☐ / ☐☐ / ☐☐ through ☐☐ / ☐☐ / ☐☐

VACCINATION RECORD

☐☐ / ☐☐	Type	Information
Month Day		

☐☐ / ☐☐	Type	Information
Month Day		

☐☐ / ☐☐	Type	Information
Month Day		

☐☐ / ☐☐	Type	Information
Month Day		

MEDICATIONS

☐☐ / ☐☐	Type	Information
Month Day		

☐☐ / ☐☐	Type	Information
Month Day		

☐☐ / ☐☐	Type	Information
Month Day		

MALFUNCTIONS

☐☐ / ☐☐	Type	Information
Month Day		

☐☐ / ☐☐	Type	Information
Month Day		

☐☐ / ☐☐	Type	Information
Month Day		

Grooming is an excellent time to examine your dog for irritated skin, lumps, bumps, ticks, fleas, and any other problems that might require veterinary attention.

DATE ☐☐ / ☐☐ / ☐☐ through ☐☐ / ☐☐ / ☐☐

VACCINATION RECORD

| ☐☐ / ☐☐ | Type | Information |
| Month / Day | | |

| ☐☐ / ☐☐ | Type | Information |
| Month / Day | | |

| ☐☐ / ☐☐ | Type | Information |
| Month / Day | | |

| ☐☐ / ☐☐ | Type | Information |
| Month / Day | | |

MEDICATIONS

| ☐☐ / ☐☐ | Type | Information |
| Month / Day | | |

| ☐☐ / ☐☐ | Type | Information |
| Month / Day | | |

| ☐☐ / ☐☐ | Type | Information |
| Month / Day | | |

MALFUNCTIONS

| ☐☐ / ☐☐ | Type | Information |
| Month / Day | | |

| ☐☐ / ☐☐ | Type | Information |
| Month / Day | | |

| ☐☐ / ☐☐ | Type | Information |
| Month / Day | | |

Do not "free feed"—that is, leave a bowl of food sitting out all day so that the canine can serve itself. This may lead to obesity. Pick a time to offer a meal, present the food, then, after perhaps half an hour, put away the bowl until the next feeding. Twice-daily feedings (once in the morning, once in the evening) will suffice for most models.

VACCINATION RECORD

☐☐ / ☐☐	Type	Information
Month Day		
☐☐ / ☐☐	Type	Information
Month Day		
☐☐ / ☐☐	Type	Information
Month Day		
☐☐ / ☐☐	Type	Information
Month Day		

MEDICATIONS

☐☐ / ☐☐	Type	Information
Month Day		
☐☐ / ☐☐	Type	Information
Month Day		
☐☐ / ☐☐	Type	Information
Month Day		

MALFUNCTIONS

☐☐ / ☐☐	Type	Information
Month Day		
☐☐ / ☐☐	Type	Information
Month Day		
☐☐ / ☐☐	Type	Information
Month Day		

Very young children should never, under any circumstances, be left alone with a dog—even a dog that knows them and has shown no aggressive tendencies.

VACCINATION RECORD

☐☐ / ☐☐	Type	Information
Month / Day		

☐☐ / ☐☐	Type	Information
Month / Day		

☐☐ / ☐☐	Type	Information
Month / Day		

☐☐ / ☐☐	Type	Information
Month / Day		

MEDICATIONS

☐☐ / ☐☐	Type	Information
Month / Day		

☐☐ / ☐☐	Type	Information
Month / Day		

☐☐ / ☐☐	Type	Information
Month / Day		

MALFUNCTIONS

☐☐ / ☐☐	Type	Information
Month / Day		

☐☐ / ☐☐	Type	Information
Month / Day		

☐☐ / ☐☐	Type	Information
Month / Day		

A very sedentary dog may need 30 percent fewer calories than an average dog of the same size. Very active dogs may require 40 to 50 percent more calories than an average dog.

YEAR 15

DATE ☐☐ / ☐☐ / ☐☐ through ☐☐ / ☐☐ / ☐☐

VACCINATION RECORD

☐☐ / ☐☐
Month / Day
Type

Information

☐☐ / ☐☐
Month / Day
Type

Information

☐☐ / ☐☐
Month / Day
Type

Information

☐☐ / ☐☐
Month / Day
Type

Information

MEDICATIONS

☐☐ / ☐☐
Month / Day
Type

Information

☐☐ / ☐☐
Month / Day
Type

Information

☐☐ / ☐☐
Month / Day
Type

Information

MALFUNCTIONS

☐☐ / ☐☐
Month / Day
Type

Information

☐☐ / ☐☐
Month / Day
Type

Information

☐☐ / ☐☐
Month / Day
Type

Information

Canines can gauge your mood by the tone of your voice, so saying something—anything—with an angry tone will usually elicit a fearful or submissive response. Likewise, saying "bad dog" in a cheerful voice will not achieve the desired effect.

VACCINATION RECORD

☐☐ Month / ☐☐ Day	**Type**	**Information**
☐☐ Month / ☐☐ Day	**Type**	**Information**
☐☐ Month / ☐☐ Day	**Type**	**Information**
☐☐ Month / ☐☐ Day	**Type**	**Information**

MEDICATIONS

☐☐ Month / ☐☐ Day	**Type**	**Information**
☐☐ Month / ☐☐ Day	**Type**	**Information**
☐☐ Month / ☐☐ Day	**Type**	**Information**

MALFUNCTIONS

☐☐ Month / ☐☐ Day	**Type**	**Information**
☐☐ Month / ☐☐ Day	**Type**	**Information**
☐☐ Month / ☐☐ Day	**Type**	**Information**

A dog who is anxious tends to bark in a high pitch; a dog who is warning off an intruder barks in a lower pitch. Warning barks may become more rapid as a stranger gets closer.

VACCINATION RECORD

| ☐☐ / ☐☐ | Type | Information |
| Month / Day | | |

| ☐☐ / ☐☐ | Type | Information |
| Month / Day | | |

| ☐☐ / ☐☐ | Type | Information |
| Month / Day | | |

| ☐☐ / ☐☐ | Type | Information |
| Month / Day | | |

MEDICATIONS

| ☐☐ / ☐☐ | Type | Information |
| Month / Day | | |

| ☐☐ / ☐☐ | Type | Information |
| Month / Day | | |

| ☐☐ / ☐☐ | Type | Information |
| Month / Day | | |

MALFUNCTIONS

| ☐☐ / ☐☐ | Type | Information |
| Month / Day | | |

| ☐☐ / ☐☐ | Type | Information |
| Month / Day | | |

| ☐☐ / ☐☐ | Type | Information |
| Month / Day | | |

If your dog is accustomed to being indoors, do not leave it outdoors and unattended for long periods. Such animals may develop severe emotional problems, become excessively dirty, and/or injure themselves.

DATE ☐☐ / ☐☐ / ☐☐ through ☐☐ / ☐☐ / ☐☐

VACCINATION RECORD

☐☐ / ☐☐	Type	Information
Month / Day		
☐☐ / ☐☐	Type	Information
Month / Day		
☐☐ / ☐☐	Type	Information
Month / Day		
☐☐ / ☐☐	Type	Information
Month / Day		

MEDICATIONS

☐☐ / ☐☐	Type	Information
Month / Day		
☐☐ / ☐☐	Type	Information
Month / Day		
☐☐ / ☐☐	Type	Information
Month / Day		

MALFUNCTIONS

☐☐ / ☐☐	Type	Information
Month / Day		
☐☐ / ☐☐	Type	Information
Month / Day		
☐☐ / ☐☐	Type	Information
Month / Day		

Suddenly switching a dog's food can lead to stomach upset and diarrhea. To avoid this, change the product gradually. On the first day, mix three parts of the current food with one part of the new food. On the next day, mix them evenly. On the third day, offer three-fourths new food. Then switch entirely to the new product.

YEAR 19

DATE ☐☐ / ☐☐ / ☐☐ through ☐☐ / ☐☐ / ☐☐

VACCINATION RECORD

☐☐ / ☐☐	Type	Information
Month / Day		

☐☐ / ☐☐	Type	Information
Month / Day		

☐☐ / ☐☐	Type	Information
Month / Day		

☐☐ / ☐☐	Type	Information
Month / Day		

MEDICATIONS

☐☐ / ☐☐	Type	Information
Month / Day		

☐☐ / ☐☐	Type	Information
Month / Day		

☐☐ / ☐☐	Type	Information
Month / Day		

MALFUNCTIONS

☐☐ / ☐☐	Type	Information
Month / Day		

☐☐ / ☐☐	Type	Information
Month / Day		

☐☐ / ☐☐	Type	Information
Month / Day		

Dogs sleep roughly 14 hours a day. Older or larger dogs (such as Saint Bernards or Newfoundlands) will sleep even more. Instead of sleeping in one continuous stretch—as most humans do—dogs will take naps of varying lengths throughout the day.

YEAR 20

DATE ☐☐ / ☐☐ / ☐☐ through ☐☐ / ☐☐ / ☐☐

VACCINATION RECORD

☐☐ / ☐☐	Type	Information
Month Day		

☐☐ / ☐☐	Type	Information
Month Day		

☐☐ / ☐☐	Type	Information
Month Day		

☐☐ / ☐☐	Type	Information
Month Day		

MEDICATIONS

☐☐ / ☐☐	Type	Information
Month Day		

☐☐ / ☐☐	Type	Information
Month Day		

☐☐ / ☐☐	Type	Information
Month Day		

MALFUNCTIONS

☐☐ / ☐☐	Type	Information
Month Day		

☐☐ / ☐☐	Type	Information
Month Day		

☐☐ / ☐☐	Type	Information
Month Day		

The operational life span of dogs averages 12 years, but your model's mileage may vary. As a rule of thumb, larger varieties depreciate much more rapidly than compact ones. For instance, a 7-year-old mastiff or Great Dane is very close to obsolescence. However, a poodle, beagle, or similar small dog could easily function twice that long or longer. The oldest documented canine life span was 29 years.

NOTES AND OBSERVATIONS

[Appendices]

AUDIO CUES: Audible dog communication typically assumes one of the following forms.

HOWLS: Wolves howl to locate other pack members over long distances. Many domestic dogs have kept this behavior. It can sometimes be initiated by sounds such as police sirens.

GROWLS: This sound is often associated with aggression, threats, and displays of dominance. However, dogs may growl during play as well. Study the dog's body language to distinguish one from the other.

GRUNTS: These are often heard when dogs greet humans or other dogs. They are the equivalent of a human sigh.

WHINES: A form of communication over intermediate distances that can signal anything from pain to submission to happiness at meeting someone.

BARKS: As with howling, these can be used to get attention, to raise the alarm, or to identify an individual. A dog who is anxious tends to bark in a high pitch; a dog who is warning off an intruder barks at a lower pitch. Warning barks may become more rapid as a stranger gets closer.

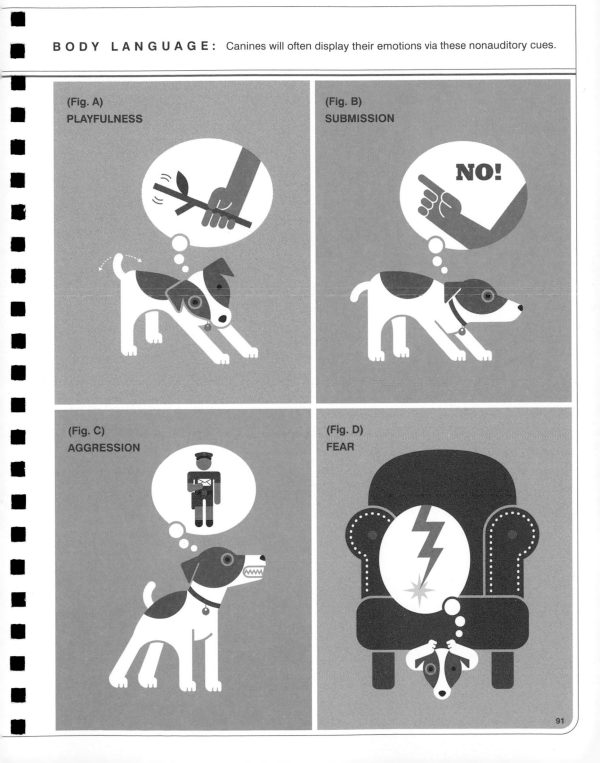

(Fig. A)
PLAYFULNESS

(Fig. B)
SUBMISSION

(Fig. C)
AGGRESSION

(Fig. D)
FEAR

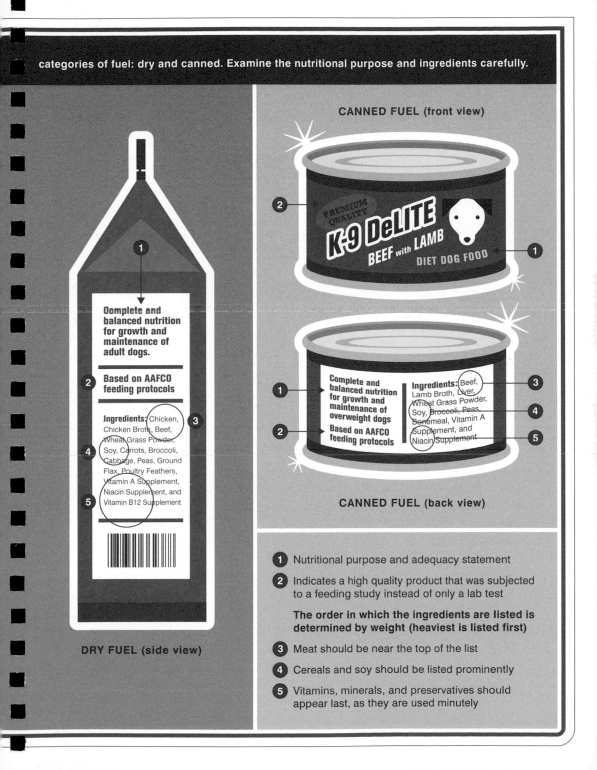

CANNED FUEL (front view)

2

PREMIUM QUALITY

K-9 DeLITE

BEEF with LAMB

DIET DOG FOOD

1

DRY FUEL (side view)

Oomplete and balanced nutrition for growth and maintenance of adult dogs.

Based on AAFCO feeding protocols

Ingredients: Chicken, Chicken Broth, Beef, Wheat Grass Powder, Soy, Carrots, Broccoli, Cabbage, Peas, Ground Flax, Poultry Feathers, Vitamin A Supplement, Niacin Supplement, and Vitamin B12 Supplement

CANNED FUEL (back view)

Complete and balanced nutrition for growth and maintenance of overweight dogs

Based on AAFCO feeding protocols

Ingredients: Beef, Lamb Broth, Liver, Wheat Grass Powder, Soy, Broccoli, Peas, Bonemeal, Vitamin A Supplement, and Niacin Supplement

1 Nutritional purpose and adequacy statement

2 Indicates a high quality product that was subjected to a feeding study instead of only a lab test

The order in which the ingredients are listed is determined by weight (heaviest is listed first)

3 Meat should be near the top of the list

4 Cereals and soy should be listed prominently

5 Vitamins, minerals, and preservatives should appear last, as they are used minutely

Calculating Age in Dog Years

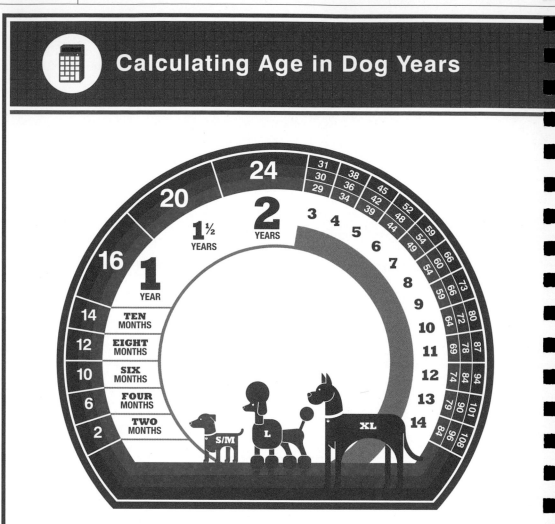

A popular misconception is that dogs age 7 years for each calendar year. In fact, canine aging is much more rapid during the first 2 years of a dog's life. After the first 2 years the ratio settles down to 5 to 1 for small and medium breeds. For large breeds the rate is 6 to 1, and for giant breeds the rate is 7 to 1. Thus, at 10 years of age a Great Dane would be 80 years old while a pug would only be 64.

Technical Support

The following organizations offer valuable information and/or services to dog owners.

Animal Poison Control Center (888) 426-4435

Run by the American Society for the Prevention of Cruelty to Animals (ASPCA), the Animal Poison Control Center is staffed 24 hours a day, 7 days a week by veterinarians. They can advise during poison emergencies, provide treatment protocols, and even consult with clients' personal veterinarians. There may be a charge for the service, depending on the circumstances, so have your credit card ready.

1-800-Save-A-Pet.com

(800) 728-3273

A national, nonprofit clearinghouse for mixed and purebred dogs in need of homes. Web-based search service allows for the easy location of rescue groups in particular areas.

American Animal Hospital Association

Member Service Center

(800) 883-6301

Can provide information on AAHA-approved veterinary hospitals in your area. For more information visit www.healthypet.com.

American Kennel Club

AKC Breeder Referral Service

(900) 407-7877

For a free Dog Buyer's Educational Packet, call AKC Customer Service at (919) 233-9767. For information on breed rescue organizations throughout the United States, visit www.akc.org/breeds/rescue.cfm.

AKC Companion Animal Recovery

(800) 252-7894

E-mail contact: found@akc.org

A 24-hour hotline to which owners of dogs with microchip identification can report their lost canines and/or receive information about their whereabouts.

American Society for the Prevention of Cruelty to Animals

(212) 876-7700

Founded in 1866, the ASPCA is the oldest humane organization in the Western Hemisphere. Among many other things, it provides humane education, advice on obtaining medical services, and support for animal shelters.

American Veterinary Medical Association

(847) 925-8070

www.avma.org

A not-for-profit association of roughly 70,000 veterinarians that can provide information on AVMA-accredited facilities in your area.

Humane Society of the United States

(202) 452-1100

www.hsus.org

Animal advocacy and information clearinghouse covering such topics as pet adoption, care, and rights.

National Pesticide Information Center

(800) 858-378

Offers free information about the toxicity of common compounds such as lawn care and gardening products.

Petswelcome.com

Extensive Internet site offering comprehensive information on traveling with dogs, including listings of hotels that allow pets; kennels; amusement park pet facilities; and how to cope with emergencies on the road.

Creating a Repair Kit

While most medical issues should be taken to a veterinarian, some minor problems can be handled at home using the following equipment. Place all these items in one container (a small, plastic toolbox is ideal) and position it someplace easily accessible. Include the name and phone number of your veterinarian, along with the phone number of the nearest animal emergency clinic.

The first-aid kit should contain:

- ❏ Roll cotton and cotton balls
- ❏ Eyewash
- ❏ Ice pack
- ❏ Gauze pads and gauze tape
- ❏ Oral syringes
- ❏ Thermometer (digital only)
- ❏ Surgical tape
- ❏ Large towels
- ❏ Medication
- ❏ Scissors
- ❏ Exam gloves
- ❏ Pill gun